LARGO DESOLATO

D1500225

LARGO DESOLATO

A play in seven scenes

VACLAV HAVEL

English version by
TOM STOPPARD

faber and faber
LONDON · BOSTON

First published in Great Britain in 1987
by Faber and Faber Limited
3 Queen Square London WC1N 3AU
Originally published by
Rowohtt Taschenbuch Verlag Gmbh,
Reinbeck bei Hamburg

Photoset by Wilmaset Birkenhead Wirral
Printed in Great Britain by
Redwood Burn Ltd Trowbridge Wiltshire

British Library Cataloguing in Publication Data

Havel, Vaclav
Largo desolato.
I. Title II. Stoppard, Tom
891.8'625 PG5039.18.A9

ISBN 0-571-13777-6

Author's dedication
for Tom Stoppard

The first production of this English text was at the Bristol Old Vic on 9 October 1986 when the cast was as follows:

PROFESSOR LEOPOLD NETTLES	John McEnery
SUZANA	Amanda Murray
LUCY	Meg Davies
EDWARD	Michael Bangerter
BERTRAM	Barrie Cookson
MARGUERITE	Edita Brychta
FIRST CHAP AND SECOND SIDNEY	Pavel Douglas
SECOND CHAP AND FIRST SIDNEY	Robert Hamilton

Directed by Claude Whatham

The naming of the characters, who needless to say have Czech names in the original, follows the Anglicization used in Bristol. For reasons which were initially to do with economics, the two 'Sidneys' and the two 'Chaps' were played by the same actors. This is not Havel's intention, although it was done with his permission.

CHARACTERS

PROFESSOR LEOPOLD NETTLES
EDWARD
SUZANA
FIRST SIDNEY
SECOND SIDNEY
LUCY
BERTRAM
FIRST CHAP
SECOND CHAP
FIRST MAN
SECOND MAN
MARGUERITE

The whole play takes place in Leopold's and Suzana's living room. It is a spacious room and all the other rooms in the flat lead off it. On the left there is the front door of the flat. The door has a peep-hole. In the back wall, on the left, there is a glass-panelled door leading to a balcony. In the middle of the wall there is a glass-panelled door leading to the kitchen. To the right of that there is a small staircase leading to the door of Suzana's room. On the right hand side, opposite the front door, there is a door leading to the bathroom, and a further door leading to Leopold's room. Between the doors the walls are covered with bookcases and bookshelves. There is a hat-stand near the front door. In the right hand half of the room there is a sofa with a low table in front of it, and a few chairs. On the table there is a large bottle of rum and a glass which LEOPOLD keeps filling up throughout the play and from which he keeps sipping. This is an old and solidly bourgeois apartment but the furnishings indicate that the occupant is an intellectual. Impressive orchestral music is heard at the beginning and the end of the play and also during the intervals between the scenes.

SCENE ONE

As the music dies away the curtain rises slowly.

LEOPOLD *is alone on the stage. He is sitting on the sofa and staring at the front door. After a long pause he gets up and looks through the peep-hole. Then he puts his ear to the door and listens intently. After another long pause the curtain drops suddenly and at the same time the music returns.*

SCENE TWO

As the music dies away the curtain rises slowly.

LEOPOLD *is alone on the stage. He is sitting on the sofa and staring at the front door. After a long pause he gets up and looks through the peep-hole. Then he puts his ear to the door and listens intently. After another long pause the curtain drops suddenly and at the same time the music returns.*

SCENE THREE

As the music dies down the curtain rises slowly.

LEOPOLD *is alone on the stage. He is sitting on the sofa and staring at the front door. After a long pause he gets up, goes to the door and looks through the peep-hole and then he puts his ear to the door and listens intently. He evidently hears something which makes him jump back. At the same moment the door bell rings.* LEOPOLD *hesitates for a moment and then cautiously approaches the door and looks through the peep-hole. That calms him and he opens the door.*
EDWARD *enters.*
LEOPOLD: At last!
EDWARD: Has anything happened?
LEOPOLD: No – *
EDWARD: Were you worried?

Translator's footnote: the use of dashes rather than full stops at the end of speeches is Havel's punctuation.

LEOPOLD: I feel better when there's someone here. Come in –
   (EDWARD *comes forward.* LEOPOLD *closes the door behind him.*)
   What's it like outside?
EDWARD: Stifling –
LEOPOLD: Lots of people?
EDWARD: No more than usual –
   (EDWARD *goes to the door leading to the balcony.*)
EDWARD: Do you mind if I open it a bit?
LEOPOLD: Go ahead –
   (EDWARD *opens the balcony door wide.*)
   What will you have?
EDWARD: Thanks, nothing for the moment –
   (LEOPOLD *sits down on the sofa.* EDWARD *takes a chair. A short pause.*)
   How did you sleep?
LEOPOLD: Essentially well. I would put it at six hours net. I woke up twice but only because I needed to pee –
EDWARD: No diarrhoea?
LEOPOLD: On the contrary –
EDWARD: How about dreams?
LEOPOLD: Nothing memorable, evidently. (*Pause.*) Do you mind if I close it now?
EDWARD: Leave it open for a while. (*Pause.*) So you're all right?
LEOPOLD: At first glance I would seem to have no reason to complain today. But in all honesty I couldn't assert that I'm feeling up to the mark –
EDWARD: Nervous?
LEOPOLD: Well, I'm always nervous –
EDWARD: And the shakes you had yesterday? All gone?
LEOPOLD: I'm afraid not. In fact they're worse. It's almost as though I'd caught a chill. (*He pauses suddenly.*) Is that somebody coming?
   (*They both listen quietly.*)
EDWARD: Nothing. Everything's okay –
LEOPOLD: And on top of that I've got complications – a touch of vertigo, suggestion of an upset stomach, tingling in the joints, loss of appetite, and even the possibility of constipation –

2

EDWARD: You mean you didn't go this morning?

LEOPOLD: No –

EDWARD: Are you sure it isn't just a hangover?

LEOPOLD: My condition has some similarities to a hangover but it's not a hangover, in as much as I hardly touched a drop yesterday –

EDWARD: Well, perhaps there's something wrong with you.

LEOPOLD: No, I'm afraid not –

EDWARD: Well, that's something to be grateful for isn't it?

LEOPOLD: Is it? I'd rather be ill than well like this. If only I could be sure they won't come today –

EDWARD: They can't be coming now –

LEOPOLD: Do you think so? Surely they can come any time –

(At that moment a key rattles in the lock. LEOPOLD *is startled.* SUZANA *comes in through the front door carrying a full shopping bag.)*

SUZANA: Hello –

*(*LEOPOLD *and* EDWARD *get up.)*

LEOPOLD: Hello – let me –

*(*LEOPOLD *takes the bag from* SUZANA *and carries it into the kitchen.)*

SUZANA: How is he?

EDWARD: The same –

*(*LEOPOLD *returns from the kitchen.)*

LEOPOLD: Did you get any meat?

SUZANA: Liver –

LEOPOLD: You didn't!

*(*SUZANA *is going up the stairs to her room.* LEOPOLD *approaches her.)*

Suzy –

(She stops halfway up the stairs and turns towards him.)

SUZANA: Yes?

LEOPOLD: I was up by about eight today – I felt like doing something – I was thinking of making a few notes – I had a piece of paper all ready but nothing came – I wasn't feeling up to scratch again. Those shakes I had yesterday came back – so I did a bit of tidying up, wiped out the sink, took out the rubbish, dried my towel, cleaned my comb, made

3

myself two soft boiled eggs for lunch –

SUZANA: What did you eat them with?

LEOPOLD: Well, with a teaspoon of course –

SUZANA: A silver one?

LEOPOLD: I don't know, it might have been –

SUZANA: How many times have I told you not to use the silver teaspoons for eggs – you can't get them clean properly –

LEOPOLD: Oh yes, I'm sorry, I forgot. After lunch I tried to read a bit and then Edward here turned up . . .

SUZANA: In other words, not a lot –

(*She goes up another step or two.*)

LEOPOLD: Suzana –

(*She stops and turns towards him.*)

As you've managed to get some liver why don't we have a special supper. I'll make mustard sauce, open a bottle of decent wine – we'll ask Lucy as well, and I'm sure Edward would join us. I think it would be good for me to let my hair down, take my mind off things, reminisce a little . . .

SUZANA: I'm sorry, Leopold, but I've got tickets for the cinema –

LEOPOLD: How about after the cinema?

SUZANA: That's too late for me – you know I've got to be up early –

(SUZANA *goes into her room.* LEOPOLD *stands for a moment looking after her awkwardly, then returns slowly to his place, and sits down. Another pause*)

LEOPOLD: Edward –

EDWARD: Yes?

LEOPOLD: Will you think of me?

EDWARD: When?

LEOPOLD: Well, when I'm there –

EDWARD: You mustn't keep thinking about that all the time!

LEOPOLD: I don't keep thinking about it all the time. It just came into my head. I'm sorry –

EDWARD: Why don't you go for a walk once in a while?

LEOPOLD: Are you mad? Go out?

EDWARD: Why not?

LEOPOLD: And be a nervous wreck the whole time, not knowing what's going on back here?

EDWARD: Nothing's going on back here –

4

LEOPOLD: I know, but how am I going to know that if I'm gadding about somewhere else? What if they came just then?

EDWARD: They'd find you weren't at home. So what?

LEOPOLD: I couldn't possibly –

(*At that moment the doorbell rings.* LEOPOLD *jumps up in confusion.* EDWARD *gets up as well.* LEOPOLD *goes to the peep-hole and looks through it and then turns towards* EDWARD.)

LEOPOLD: (*Whispering*) What did I tell you!

EDWARD: (*Whispering*) Is it them?

(LEOPOLD *nods. They pause, at a loss. The bell rings again.*)

LEOPOLD: (*Whispering*) Should I open the door?

EDWARD: (*Whispering*) Yes, you have to –

(LEOPOLD *hesitates a moment, then breathes in, goes to the door and opens it decisively. The newcomers are* FIRST SIDNEY *and* SECOND SIDNEY.)

FIRST SIDNEY: Good afternoon, sir –

LEOPOLD: Good afternoon –

SECOND SIDNEY: Can we come in?

LEOPOLD: Do . . .

(FIRST SIDNEY *and* SECOND SIDNEY *come forward a few paces.* LEOPOLD *closes the door behind them. They all remain standing and looking at each other somewhat at a loss.*)

FIRST SIDNEY: You don't remember us?

LEOPOLD: I can't place you at the moment –

FIRST SIDNEY: We called on you once before, two years ago. You've obviously forgotten. I'm Sidney and he's also Sidney –

LEOPOLD: How do you do –

SECOND SIDNEY: We won't hold you up long –

LEOPOLD: (*Perplexed*) Well, do sit down –

(*They all sit down,* LEOPOLD *on the sofa, the others on the chairs.*)

FIRST SIDNEY: Is it all right to smoke?

LEOPOLD: Yes – certainly –

FIRST SIDNEY: Actually, I don't smoke myself; I was asking for Sidney here, he smokes like a chimney –

(SECOND SIDNEY *is going through his pockets but can't find*

5

any cigarettes. LEOPOLD *offers him one.* SECOND SIDNEY *takes one and lights it. There is an awkward pause.*)
Do you need any paper?

LEOPOLD: Do you mean for writing on?

SECOND SIDNEY: If you need any we can get you some –

LEOPOLD: Really?

FIRST SIDNEY: Seeing as we work in a paper mill –

LEOPOLD: You do?

SECOND SIDNEY: So no problem –

(*Pause.* SUZANA *comes out of her room and down the stairs.*)

LEOPOLD: Suzana, these gentlemen are from the paper mill. It seems they've been here before –

SUZANA: Good afternoon –

FIRST SIDNEY: Good afternoon –

(SUZANA *beckons to* EDWARD *who gets up and goes with her to the kitchen. During the following scene both of them can be seen through the glass-panelled door taking out various foodstuffs from the shopping bag, putting them where they belong and, during all this time, either discussing something in a lively way or perhaps quarrelling. Pause*)
Oh, by the way, we've got a lot of interesting stuff from the mill – minutes of meetings and so on – I'm sure you'd find it interesting –

LEOPOLD: I'm sure I would –

SECOND SIDNEY: We'll bring it you –

(*Pause*)

FIRST SIDNEY: We know everything –

LEOPOLD: Every what thing?

FIRST SIDNEY: About you –

LEOPOLD: I see –

SECOND SIDNEY: What Sidney is trying to say is, we're your fans. Not just us either –

LEOPOLD: Thank you –

FIRST SIDNEY: There's lots of people looking to you –

LEOPOLD: Thank you –

SECOND SIDNEY: We all believe that it will all turn out right for you in the end –

LEOPOLD: Well, I'm not sure –

6

SECOND SIDNEY: The main thing is that you mustn't weaken –
we need you and we believe in you – you being the man you
are –

LEOPOLD: Thank you –
(*Pause.*)

FIRST SIDNEY: We're not holding you up, are we?

LEOPOLD: No –

FIRST SIDNEY: Are you sure? Because if we are, you only have to
say so and we'll push off –

LEOPOLD: You're not holding me up –
(*Pause.*)

FIRST SIDNEY: You know, I'm just an ordinary sort of bloke, a
nobody, but I can spot a few things and I've got my own
opinion and nobody can deny me that. And what I think is,
there's a lot that could be done – certainly more than is being
done at the moment –

LEOPOLD: This is it –

SECOND SIDNEY: Speaking for myself and Sidney here, we
reckon – and this is partly why we're here – to our way of
thinking not all the possibilities have been exhausted – I
would venture to say that the most promising possibilities are
still ahead of us. One has to take hold of the situation by the
scruff of the neck –

LEOPOLD: What possibilities in particular did you have in mind?

FIRST SIDNEY: Well, that would require some discussion, of
course –

LEOPOLD: Well, at least tell me what direction we ought to be
taking.

FIRST SIDNEY: Different directions all at the same time. Surely
no one knows that better than you! In short, it seems to us
that it's time to take the initiative – something that would
make them sit up.

LEOPOLD: I'm not sure that present circumstances differ
significantly from the circumstances that have prevailed up
to now, but even so I'm not *a priori* against an initiative –

FIRST SIDNEY: I'm glad we agree – who else but you could get
things going again?

LEOPOLD: Well as for *me* –

7

SECOND SIDNEY: We realize that things are probably not easy for you at the moment. But the respect in which you're held puts you under an obligation –

LEOPOLD: I know –

FIRST SIDNEY: You'll know what's best to do, after all you're a philosopher and I'm an ordinary bloke, a nobody. It goes without saying we're not forcing you – we haven't got the right, and furthermore you can't be expected to do it for everybody, all on your own, but, that said, what we think is, don't get me wrong, I'll let you have it straight, – that said, we are of the opinion that you could be doing more than you are in your place –

LEOPOLD: I'll think it over –

FIRST SIDNEY: We're only saying this because we're your fans – and not just us –

LEOPOLD: Thank you –

SECOND SIDNEY: A lot of people are looking to you –

LEOPOLD: Thank you –

FIRST SIDNEY: The main thing is that you mustn't weaken – we believe in you and we need you –

LEOPOLD: Thank you –

(*Pause.*)

SECOND SIDNEY: We're not holding you up, are we?

LEOPOLD: No –

SECOND SIDNEY: Are you sure? Because if we are you only have to say so and we'll push off –

LEOPOLD: You're not holding me up –

(*Pause.*)

SECOND SIDNEY: One could certainly do more – you just have to get hold of the situation by the scruff of the neck – and who else but you is there to get things going again?

LEOPOLD: Well, as for *me* –

FIRST SIDNEY: We have faith in you –

SECOND SIDNEY: And we need you –

LEOPOLD: Thank you –

FIRST SIDNEY: We're not holding you up, are we?

LEOPOLD: No –

FIRST SIDNEY: Are you really sure? Because if we are you only have to say so and we'll push off –

LEOPOLD: You are not holding me up. Excuse me –

(LEOPOLD *gets up and walks to the balcony door, shuts it and returns to his seat.*)

SECOND SIDNEY: The main thing is that you mustn't weaken –

LEOPOLD: (*Suddenly alert*) Just a moment –

FIRST SIDNEY: What's up?

LEOPOLD: I think somebody's coming –

SECOND SIDNEY: I can't hear anything –

FIRST SIDNEY: The respect in which you're held puts you under an obligation –

(*At that moment the doorbell rings. That startles* LEOPOLD *who gets up quickly, goes to the front door and looks through the peep-hole. He calms down and turns towards the* TWO SIDNEYS.)

LEOPOLD: A friend of mine –

(LEOPOLD *opens the door and* LUCY *comes in.*)

LUCY: Hello, Leo –

LEOPOLD: Come in, Lucy –

(LEOPOLD *closes the door and leads* LUCY *to the table.*)

LUCY: I see you've got company –

LEOPOLD: They're friends from the paper mill –

LUCY: Good afternoon –

FIRST SIDNEY: Good afternoon, miss –

LEOPOLD: Sit down –

(LUCY *sits down next to* LEOPOLD *on the sofa. There is a longer awkward pause.*)

Would you like some rum?

LUCY: You know I don't drink rum –

(*Pause.*)

LEOPOLD: How's life?

LUCY: Depressing –

LEOPOLD: Why's that?

LUCY: Loneliness.

(*Pause.*)

LEOPOLD: These gentlemen think it's time to take the initiative –

LUCY: They've got something there.

(*Awkward pause.*)

Did I come at the wrong moment? You were obviously in the middle of discussing something –

LEOPOLD: It's all right –

(*Awkward pause.*)

Have you had supper?

LUCY: No –

LEOPOLD: We're having liver. Would you like to stay?

LUCY: That would be lovely –

(*Another awkward pause.* LUCY *takes a bottle of pills out of her handbag. She puts the bottle on the table.*)

I've brought you some vitamins –

LEOPOLD: You never forget –

(*Awkward pause.*)

I'm told it's stifling today –

LUCY: Stifling and humid –

(*Awkward pause.*)

LEOPOLD: Edward opened the balcony door but I closed it again – I don't like draughts –

LUCY: Is Edward here?

LEOPOLD: Yes –

(*Awkward pause.* LEOPOLD *is becoming more and more nervous because both* FIRST *and* SECOND SIDNEY *are sitting there and not showing any signs of leaving. Several times he seems on the point of saying something but each time changes his mind. Finally he blurts out –*)

LEOPOLD: Well, look how the evening's coming on –

(LUCY *bursts out laughing.* LEOPOLD *presses her hand. Awkward pause. Both* SIDNEYS *sitting there apparently dumbfounded.*)

I've still got a few things to do –

(LUCY *bursts out laughing despite herself.*)

LUCY: What have you got to do?

(*She bursts out again and* LEOPOLD *kicks her under the table.*)

LEOPOLD: (*Stammering*) Things – make some notes – some supper –

(*He relapses into a long stifling silence. Then* SUZANA *followed by* EDWARD, *enters from the kitchen.*)

SUZANA: Lucy!

LUCY: Suzy!

(LUCY *gets up at once and goes towards* SUZANA *and they embrace.*)

Darling! How's life?

SUZANA: Never stops!

LUCY: We must have a chat – I've got so much to tell you.

SUZANA: Me too – but some other time, all right? – I'm in a rush.

LUCY: Hey, are you leaving?

SUZANA: I've got tickets for the cinema –

LUCY: What a shame – I was so looking forward to seeing you!

(FIRST SIDNEY *suddenly thumps his knees and stands up.* SECOND SIDNEY *gets up as well.* LEOPOLD *starts getting up.*)

FIRST SIDNEY: Well, we shall look in on you soon –

LEOPOLD: Fine –

SECOND SIDNEY: And we'll bring you that writing paper –

LEOPOLD: Fine –

FIRST SIDNEY: And also the stuff from the paper mill –

LEOPOLD: Fine –

SECOND SIDNEY: The main thing is – keep your chin up!

LEOPOLD: Thank you –

FIRST SIDNEY: When are you expecting them?

LEOPOLD: All the time –

SECOND SIDNEY: We're with you – stick with it! So long –

LEOPOLD: So long –

LUCY: So long –

(LEOPOLD *accompanies the* SIDNEYS *to the front door and opens the door for them. They go out.* LEOPOLD *closes the door behind them, and, completely spent, leans back against the door.*)

May I ask, who that was?

LEOPOLD: I don't know. They wanted something from me. I'm not sure what. I'm sure they mean well –

SUZANA: That sort of thing happens all the time round here – but I have to run. (*To* EDWARD) Let's go! (*To* LUCY) Bye for now –

LUCY: Bye, Suzy –

EDWARD: Bye –

(SUZANA *and* EDWARD *leave.* LUCY *and* LEOPOLD *are left alone.* LUCY *smiles at* LEOPOLD *for a moment, then takes hold of his hands, pulls him towards her and kisses him.*)

LUCY: Do you love me?

LEOPOLD: Mm.

LUCY: Really?

LEOPOLD: Really –

LUCY: Well why don't you say so sometimes without being asked? You've never once!

LEOPOLD: As you know, I avoid off-the-peg expressions –

LUCY: The simple truth is, you're ashamed of loving me!

LEOPOLD: Phenomenology has taught me always to beware of the propositional statement that lies outside demonstrable experience. I prefer to say less than I feel rather than to risk saying more –

LUCY: You think loving me is not a demonstrable experience?

LEOPOLD: We may mean different things by the word love. Perhaps, though the difference may be small the word denotes, for me, something on a higher plane than for you – Just a minute!

(LEOPOLD *leaves* LUCY *to approach the front door and looks through the peep-hole.*)

LUCY: What is it?

LEOPOLD: I thought I heard someone coming –

LUCY: I can't hear anything –

(LEOPOLD *comes back from the door and turns towards her.*)

LEOPOLD: Forgive me, Lucy, but does our love have to consist solely in this endless examination of itself?

LUCY: What do you expect when you're so evasive all the time –

LEOPOLD: It's just that like all women you long for security and men look for something higher –

LUCY: Just my luck to keep picking lovers with a permanent crick in their neck –

LEOPOLD: Don't be disgusting!

LUCY: What do you mean?

LEOPOLD: Please don't use the word lover! At least don't apply it to me –

12

LUCY: Why?

LEOPOLD: It's disgusting –

LUCY: Why?

LEOPOLD: It turns man into nothing but an ever-naked prick –

LUCY: (*Laughing*) Oh, who's being disgusting now –

LEOPOLD: Why don't you sit down?

> (LUCY *sits down on the sofa.*)
> Can I get you anything?

LUCY: Is there any wine?

LEOPOLD: I'll get some –

> (LEOPOLD *goes into the kitchen and after a moment returns with a bottle of wine, a bottle opener and two glasses. He opens the bottle, pours wine into both glasses, takes one and* LUCY *takes the other.*)
> Well, cheers!

LUCY: Cheers!

> (*They both take a drink.* LEOPOLD *sits down on the sofa next to her. Pause.*)
> So tell me –

LEOPOLD: What?

LUCY: What did you do today?

LEOPOLD: I don't know –

LUCY: Did you write?

LEOPOLD: I wanted to but it wouldn't come. I wasn't feeling well –

LUCY: Did you have your depression again?

LEOPOLD: That was another thing –

LUCY: You won't get rid of it till you start writing. Everybody's waiting for your new piece –

LEOPOLD: That's just the trouble –

LUCY: But you had it all worked out –

LEOPOLD: What do you mean?

LUCY: Well, just what you were telling me – that love is actually a dimension of being – it gives fulfilment and meaning to existence –

LEOPOLD: I couldn't have made it sound like such a cliché –

LUCY: No doubt you put it better –

LEOPOLD: It's funny but when I run out of excuses for putting off writing and make up my mind to start, I stumble over the first banality – pencil or pen? – which paper? – and then this thing starts –

LUCY: What thing?

LEOPOLD: The cycle thing –

LUCY: What's that?

LEOPOLD: My thoughts just start going round in a loop –

LUCY: Hm –

LEOPOLD: Look, do we have to talk about me?

LUCY: You love to talk about yourself!

LEOPOLD: That's just what you think –

(LUCY *puts her head on* LEOPOLD'*s shoulder. He embraces her but they both continue to look straight ahead, absorbed in thought. Pause.*)

LUCY: Leopold –

LEOPOLD: Yes –

LUCY: I can help you break out of that –

LEOPOLD: How?

LUCY: You need love – real love – mad passionate love – not that theoretical one, the one you write about –

LEOPOLD: I'm a bit old for that –

LUCY: You're not old, it's just that you've got an emotional block – but I'll unblock you –

(LUCY *embraces* LEOPOLD *and begins to kiss his face.* LEOPOLD *sits perplexed and remains quite passive. The curtain falls and the music returns.*)

SCENE FOUR

The music fades and the curtain rises slowly.

It is late in the evening. It is dark behind the balcony door.

BERTRAM *is sitting on the sofa.* LEOPOLD, *who is standing in the background by the balcony door, wears a dressing gown with nothing underneath it, and he is rather dishevelled and seems to be cold.*

BERTRAM: How long is it since you went out?

LEOPOLD: I don't know – ages –

BERTRAM: You don't go out at all then?

14

LEOPOLD: No –
  (*Pause.*)
BERTRAM: How much do you drink?
LEOPOLD: The same as everyone else –
BERTRAM: Starting in the morning?
LEOPOLD: As the case may be –
  (*Pause.*)
BERTRAM: How do you sleep?
LEOPOLD: It varies –
BERTRAM: Do you ever dream about them? Or dream that you're already there?
LEOPOLD: Sometimes –
  (*Pause.*)
BERTRAM: Leopold –
LEOPOLD: Yes?
BERTRAM: You don't doubt, do you, that we all like you –
LEOPOLD: I know –
LUCY: (*Off stage*) Leopold –
LEOPOLD: (*Calls out*) Just a minute –
  (*Pause.* LEOPOLD *is trembling with cold and rubbing his arms.* BERTRAM *looks through the medicines lying on the table.*)
BERTRAM: Vitamins?
LEOPOLD: Yes –
BERTRAM: Apart from vitamins are you on anything else?
LEOPOLD: Not really – why do you ask?
BERTRAM: There's some talk –
LEOPOLD: What sort of talk?
BERTRAM: Forget it –
  (*Pause.*)
BERTRAM: Quite a few people complain that you never answer letters –
LEOPOLD: I was never much of a letter writer –
BERTRAM: Well, there's no law about it . . . still, it's a pity that it lends support to the rumours –
LEOPOLD: What rumours?
BERTRAM: That you're no longer reliable, so –
LEOPOLD: I reply to anything important – perhaps something got lost in the post somewhere –

(*Pause.*)

BERTRAM: What did you think of that collection?

LEOPOLD: What collection?

BERTRAM: The stuff I lent you the other day –

LEOPOLD: Ah yes –

BERTRAM: Have you read it?

LEOPOLD: To tell you the truth –

BERTRAM: It's essential reading –

LEOPOLD: I know – That's exactly why I couldn't just glance through it – There's a mood for everything – I can't just read anything any time –
(*Pause.*)

BERTRAM: Leopold –

LEOPOLD: Yes?

BERTRAM: You don't doubt, do you, that we all like you?

LEOPOLD: I know –

LUCY: (*Off stage*) Leopold –

LEOPOLD: (*Calls out*) Just a minute –
(*Pause.* LEOPOLD *is trembling with cold and rubbing his arms.*)

BERTRAM: Leopold –

LEOPOLD: Yes?

BERTRAM: It goes without saying it's your own business –

LEOPOLD: What is?

BERTRAM: You don't have to account to me –

LEOPOLD: What?

BERTRAM: I'm asking as a friend –

LEOPOLD: I know –

BERTRAM: Is it true that you're seeing Lucy?

LEOPOLD: It's not that simple –

BERTRAM: And how are things between you and Suzana?

LEOPOLD: We get along –
(*Pause.*)

BERTRAM: Leopold –

LEOPOLD: Yes?

BERTRAM: You don't doubt, do you, that we all like you?

LEOPOLD: I know –
(*Pause.*)

LUCY: (*Off stage*) Leopold –

LEOPOLD: (*Calls out*) Just a minute –
  (*Pause.* LEOPOLD *is trembling with cold and is rubbing his arms.*)

BERTRAM: It's terrible of course to live with this nerve-racking uncertainty – we all understand that. None of us knows how we'd stand it ourselves. That's why so many people are concerned about you. You have to understand that –

LEOPOLD: I do understand –

BERTRAM: I'm not just speaking for myself – I'm really here on behalf of everyone –

LEOPOLD: Who's everyone?

BERTRAM: Your friends –

LEOPOLD: Are you an emissary?

BERTRAM: If you want to call it that –

LEOPOLD: And what are you concerned about, specifically?

BERTRAM: How shall I put it? I don't want to be hard on you or hurt you in any way but on the other hand I wouldn't be acting as your friend if I were to be less than frank –

LEOPOLD: And what are you concerned about, specifically?

BERTRAM: How should I put it? It's not simply a general issue, it's mostly about you personally –

LEOPOLD: And what are you concerned about, specifically?

BERTRAM: How should I put it? Simply, there's growing circumstantial evidence giving rise to certain speculations –

LEOPOLD: What circumstantial evidence? What speculations?

BERTRAM: Your friends – and I won't deny I include myself – we've all – for some time – and let's hope our fears are groundless – we've all – for some time – begun to question whether you might not crack under the strain – whether you'll be able to meet all the claims which, thanks to all you've done already – the claims which are made on you – that you'll be able to fulfil the expectations which – forgive me – are rightly expected of you – if you'll be, in short, up to your mission, which is to do justice to those great obligations, to the truth, to the world, to everyone for whom you set an example – set by your own work – forgive me – but quite simply we are beginning to be slightly afraid

17

that you might let us down and in so doing bring upon
yourself – forgive me – it would be bound to be so, given
your sensitivity – bring upon yourself endless agony –
(*Short pause.*)
You're not angry, are you, that I'm speaking so openly?

LEOPOLD: No – on the contrary –
(*Pause.*)

LUCY: (*Off stage*) Leopold –

LEOPOLD: (*Calls out*) Just a minute –
(*Pause.* LEOPOLD *is trembling with cold and is rubbing his
arms.*)

BERTRAM: It's terrible, of course, to live with this nerve-racking
uncertainty. We all understand that. None of us knows how
we'd stand it ourselves. That's why so many people are
concerned about you. You have to understand that –

LEOPOLD: I do understand –

BERTRAM: The more they count on you the harder it would be
for them if you failed to hold out in some way –

LEOPOLD: People are calling on me all the time – not long ago a
couple of lads from the paper mill showed up – typical
workers – ordinary people –

BERTRAM: That's certainly excellent, but, how should I put it?

LEOPOLD: What?

BERTRAM: How should I put it?

LEOPOLD: How should you put what?

BERTRAM: The question is whether a visit from a couple of
paper-mill workers – excellent though it is in itself – is
simply – or might become simply – forgive me – a kind of
inaction in action – a leftover from a world which is no
longer the case – whether you might not be playing the role
in a mechanical, superficial way to reassure yourself that
you are still the person to whom that role properly
belonged. What is at stake here is that a gap should not
open up between you and your role in society, so that your
role, which was a true reflection of your personality,
becomes a crutch to prop you up – circumstantial evidence
of a supposed continuity of personality – but spurious,
illusory, self-deceiving – by means of which you try to

assure the world and yourself that you are still the person
who you in fact no longer are – in short, that your role
which grew naturally out of your attitudes and your work
should not become a mere substitute, and that you don't
attach to that role, which has long since kept going
autonomously, on its own momentum, don't attach to it the
sole and lasting proof of your moral existence, and thus let
your entire human identity hang on a visit from a couple of
know-nothing workers from the paper mill –
(*Short pause.*)
You're not angry, are you, that I'm speaking so openly?
LEOPOLD: No – on the contrary –
(*Pause.*)
LUCY: (*Off stage*) Leopold –
LEOPOLD: (*Calls out*) Just a minute –
(*Pause.* LEOPOLD *is trembling with cold and rubbing his
arms.*)
BERTRAM: It's terrible of course to live with this nerve-racking
uncertainty. We all understand that. None of us knows how
we'd be able to stand it ourselves. That's why so many
people are concerned about you. You have to understand
that –
LEOPOLD: I do understand –
BERTRAM: You must believe me, too, that all I wish for is that
we're worrying about nothing –
LEOPOLD: I do believe you –
BERTRAM: And even if this danger, which we your friends
worry about, is infinitesimal, I have a duty – to you, to
myself, to all of us – to confess those worries to you –
LEOPOLD: I understand –
BERTRAM: By all the things you did and have been doing up to
now, you've earned our respect and our love, and in so
doing you have suffered a great deal. Obviously you are not
a superman, and the oppressive atmosphere in which you
have had to live is bound to have left its mark. But all that
said, I can't escape the awful feeling that lately something
inside you has begun to collapse – as if an axis that has held
you together has given way, as if the ground is collapsing

under your feet – as if you've gone lame inside – that you are tending more and more to act the part of yourself instead of being yourself. Your personal life, that vital plank, is – don't be angry – in a mess, you're lacking a fixed point out of which everything inside you would grow and develop – you're losing the strength and perhaps even the will to put your affairs in order – you're erratic – you're letting yourself be tossed about by chance currents, you're sinking deeper and deeper into a void and you can't get a grip on things – you're just waiting for what is going to happen and so you're no longer the self-aware subject of your life, you're turning into its passive object – you're obviously at the mercy of great demons but they do not drive you in any direction, they merely drive about inside you – your existence seems to have become a cumbersome burden to you and you have really settled for listening helplessly to the passing of the time. What happened to your perspective on things? To your humour? Your industry and persistence? The pointedness of your observations? Your irony and self-irony? Your capacity for enthusiasm, for emotional involvement, for commitment, even for sacrifice?! I fear for you, Leopold – I fear for us! We need you! You have no idea how we need you, we need you the way you used to be! So I am asking you to swear that you won't give up – Don't weaken! Keep at it! Get a grip on yourself! Pull yourself together! Straighten up! Leopold –

LEOPOLD: Yes?

BERTRAM: You don't doubt, do you, that we all like you?

LEOPOLD: I know –

BERTRAM: So I beg you – be again that brilliant Leopold Nettles whom everybody held on high!

(*From Leopold's room* LUCY *emerges quietly, dressed only in a candlewick bedspread, naked underneath it.*)

LUCY: Bertram –

(BERTRAM *is rather startled. He gets up quickly and looks at* LUCY *in astonishment.*)

BERTRAM: Oh, Lucy –

20

LUCY: Can't you see he's cold?

BERTRAM: He never mentioned it –

LUCY: Also, it's late –

BERTRAM: Yes – of course – forgive me – I'm sorry – I didn't realize – I'm just going –

LEOPOLD: You don't have to rush – stay the night if you like –

BERTRAM: No – thank you – and so long –

LUCY: So long – and don't be offended –

BERTRAM: That's quite all right – it was presumptuous of me – so long –

LEOPOLD: Cheerio and do come again some time!

BERTRAM: Glad to –

(BERTRAM *goes out through the front door. Short pause.*)

LEOPOLD: You didn't have to push him out like that –

LUCY: He would have been sitting here all night – And I want you for myself – We get so little time –

LEOPOLD: And it's not the best thing in the world that he saw you here –

LUCY: Why?

LEOPOLD: You know how much talk there'll be now –

LUCY: So what? Or are you ashamed of me?

LEOPOLD: It's not that –

LUCY: Then why do you treat me like a stranger in front of other people?

LEOPOLD: I don't, do I?

LUCY: Yes you do! I can't remember you ever taking my hand in company – touching me – not even a fond glance –

LEOPOLD: Hadn't we better go to bed?

LUCY: No –

LEOPOLD: Why?

LUCY: Because I want to have a serious talk with you –

LEOPOLD: About our relationship?

LUCY: Yes –

LEOPOLD: In that case at least fetch me a blanket –

(LUCY *goes to Leopold's room and returns in a moment with a blanket.* LEOPOLD *sits down comfortably on the sofa and wraps himself in the blanket. Short pause.*)

LUCY: I knew it wasn't going to be easy for me – you know I

had to make a few sacrifices – and what I am trying to say –
reluctantly but I have to say it – look, I respect your
idiosyncracies –

LEOPOLD: If you mean what happened – didn't happen – I
mean in there – (*He points to his room.*) then I've already
explained that I haven't been feeling up to the mark today –

LUCY: That's not what I meant – and if we're going to talk
about it then there's other reasons behind it –

LEOPOLD: Such as?

LUCY: You're simply blocked – you're censoring yourself –
you're afraid to give in to any emotion or experience –
you're controlling, observing, watching yourself every
minute – you're thinking about it, so in the end it's duty
instead of pleasure, and then, of course, it doesn't work –
but that's my problem – I wasn't going to talk about it
now –

LEOPOLD: About what, then?

LUCY: Everything I've done for us I've done freely and
willingly, I'm not complaining and I don't want anything in
return – I only want you to admit what is true –

LEOPOLD: What do you mean?

LUCY: We're seeing each other – we're lovers – we love each
other –

LEOPOLD: Have I ever denied it?

LUCY: Forgive me but you do everything you can to deny it, to
make it invisible, to avoid acknowledging it, you behave as
if it wasn't there –

LEOPOLD: I'm possibly more reserved about some things than I
should be, but – forgive me – you're partly to blame –

LUCY: Me? How?

LEOPOLD: You know – I'm really afraid of you –

LUCY: Me?

LEOPOLD: Your ceaseless effort to give a name to our
relationship, to make your status somehow official, and the
way you defend your territory while quietly but relentlessly
trying to enlarge it – the way you have to discuss it
endlessly – all that, quite naturally, makes me defensive. By
my reserve, by wariness, perhaps even by a mild cynicism,

22

I have been compensating for a subconscious fear of being manipulated, if not actually colonized – I reproach myself bitterly for my behaviour but I can't overcome it –

LUCY: But I ask so little of you! You must see that I live only for you and through you and all I want is for you to admit to yourself that you love me!

LEOPOLD: Hm –

LUCY: And I believe you do love me! I don't believe that you are incapable of love! I don't believe that my love is incapable of awakening love even in you! I'm on your side. Without love no one is a complete person! We only achieve an identity through the person next to us! – isn't that how you put it in your *Ontology of the Human Self*?! You'll see that if you lose your ridiculous inhibitions you'll come alive again – and even your work will go better than you can imagine!

LEOPOLD: I feel sorry for you, Lucy –

LUCY: Why?

LEOPOLD: You deserve someone better. I'm just worthless –

LUCY: I don't like you talking about yourself like that –

LEOPOLD: It's true, Lucy. I can't get rid of the awful feeling that lately something has begun to collapse inside me – as if some axis which was holding me together has broken, the ground collapsing under my feet, as if I'd gone lame inside – I sometimes have the feeling that I'm acting the part of myself instead of being myself. I'm lacking a fixed point out of which I can grow and develop. I'm erratic – I'm letting myself be tossed about by chance currents – I'm sinking deeper and deeper into a void and I can no longer get a grip on things. In truth I'm just waiting for this thing that's going to happen and am no longer the self-aware subject of my own life but becoming merely its passive object – I have a feeling sometimes that all I am doing is listening helplessly to the passing of the time. What happened to my perspective on things? My humour? My industry and persistence? The pointedness of my observations? My irony and self-irony? My capacity for enthusiasm, for emotional involvement, for commitment, even for sacrifice? The

23

oppressive atmosphere in which I have been forced to live for so long is bound to have left its mark! Outwardly I go on acting my role as if nothing has happened but inside I'm no longer the person you all take me for. It's hard to admit it to myself, but if *I* can all the more reason for you to! It's a touching and beautiful thing that you don't lose hope of making me into someone better than I am but – don't be angry – it's an illusion. I've fallen apart, I'm paralysed, I won't change and it would be best if they came for me and took me where I would no longer be the cause of unhappiness and disillusion –

(LUCY *gets up, upset, goes quickly to the balcony door. She opens it and goes out on to the balcony and stands looking out into the night with her back to the room. Soon it becomes clear that she is crying.* LEOPOLD *looks at her perplexed and after a while speaks to her.*)

Lucy –

(LUCY *doesn't react. Pause.*)

There, there, Lucy, what's the matter?

(LUCY *doesn't react. Pause.* LEOPOLD *gets up and approaches her slowly, still wrapped up in a blanket.*)

Are you crying, Lucy?

(*Pause.*)

Why are you crying?

(*Pause.*)

Don't cry!

(*Pause.*)

I didn't want to upset you – I didn't realize –

(*He has approached* LUCY *and touched her carefully on the shoulder.* LUCY *with a tear-stained face turns suddenly to him and cries out.*)

LUCY: Don't touch me!

(LEOPOLD *steps back surprised.* LUCY *comes back into the room, wiping her eyes, sobbing quietly.*)

LEOPOLD: What's the matter?

LUCY: Leave me alone –

LEOPOLD: There, there – what have I done now?

LUCY: You're a worse case than I thought –

LEOPOLD: How do you mean?

LUCY: All this talk – it's nothing but excuses! You sang a different tune the first time you got me to stay with you! You said our relationship would give you back some of your lost integrity! – That it would renew your hope – that it would put you back together emotionally! – That it would open a door into a new life! You just say what suits you! No, Leopold, you're no broken wreck, you're an ordinary bullshit-artist – you've had enough of me and now you want to get shot of me – so now you paint a picture of your ruin to make me understand that there's nothing more I can expect from you and – on top of that – to make me feel sorry for you! You're ruined all right, but not in the way you say – it's your dishonesty that shows how ruined you are! And simpleton that I am, I believed that I could awaken love in you, that I'd give you back your zest for life, that I'd help you! You're beyond help! Serves me right – one great illusion less –

LEOPOLD: You're being unfair, Lucy – I really am going through a crisis – even Bertram says so –

LUCY: Please don't go on – there's no point. I'm going to get dressed –

LEOPOLD: Don't be silly, Lucy! This is no way to part –
(LEOPOLD *tries to embrace her but she breaks free from him. At that moment the doorbell rings. It startles them both and they look at each other in confusion. Their quarrel is forgotten. LEOPOLD throws his blanket on the sofa, goes quickly to the front door and looks through the peep-hole. Then, completely rattled, turns to* LUCY.)
(*Whispering*) It's them!

LUCY: (*Whispering*) What are we going to do?

LEOPOLD: (*Whispering*) I don't know – go in the bedroom – I'll let them in –

LUCY: I'm staying here with you!
(*The doorbell rings again.* LEOPOLD *breathes in, smooths his hair, goes to the door and opens it decisively. The* FIRST CHAP *and* SECOND CHAP *enter.*)

FIRST CHAP: Good evening, Professor –

25

LEOPOLD: Good evening –

FIRST CHAP: I suppose you know who we are –

LEOPOLD: I suppose so –

SECOND CHAP: You thought we wouldn't come any more today, did you?

LEOPOLD: I realize you can come any time –

FIRST CHAP: We must apologize for the intrusion – you obviously had other plans for the evening –

(*The* TWO CHAPS *smile lecherously.*)

LEOPOLD: What plans I had is my own business –

SECOND CHAP: We possibly won't keep you long, it depends on you –

FIRST CHAP: It's a pleasure to meet you. According to our colleagues you're a sensible chap so with luck we'll soon come to an understanding –

LEOPOLD: I don't know what there is to understand. I've got my things ready, I just need time to get dressed –

SECOND CHAP: What's the hurry? It may not come to the worst –

FIRST CHAP: But we must ask the lady to kindly leave –

LUCY: I'm staying!

SECOND CHAP: No, you're leaving –

(LUCY *clings on to* LEOPOLD.)

LEOPOLD: My friend can't leave now –

FIRST CHAP: Why?

LEOPOLD: She's got nowhere to go –

SECOND CHAP: In that case we'll put her up for the night.

LEOPOLD: Oh no you won't!

FIRST CHAP: Watch!

(*The* FIRST CHAP *opens the front door and makes a gesture towards the corridor. The* FIRST MAN *and the* SECOND MAN *enter smartly. The* FIRST CHAP *points towards* LUCY. *The* FIRST *and* SECOND MAN *go to her and take her by the hands.* LUCY *struggles against them and* LEOPOLD *clasps her in his arms.*)

LUCY: You bastards!

LEOPOLD: Don't touch her!

(*The* FIRST *and* SECOND MAN *pull* LUCY *out of* LEOPOLD's *embrace and drag her towards the front door.* LEOPOLD *tries to prevent them but they push him roughly away.*)

LUCY: (*Shouting*) Help!
   (FIRST *and* SECOND MAN *put their hands over Lucy's mouth and drag her out. The* FIRST CHAP *dismisses the men with a gesture and closes the door.*)

FIRST CHAP: Now that wasn't necessary was it?
   (LEOPOLD *remains silent.*)

SECOND CHAP: You don't have to worry about your girlfriend, nobody's going to harm her. As soon as she comes to her senses we'll take her home. You don't think we'd let her run around the streets in a candlewick bedspread –

FIRST CHAP: We're not inhuman, you can be sure of that –
   (LEOPOLD *closes the balcony door. He picks up his blanket and wraps himself into it and sits down rebelliously on the sofa. Short pause.*)
   Do you mind if we sit down too?
   (LEOPOLD *shrugs.* FIRST *and* SECOND CHAPS *sit down on chairs. Pause.*)
   We're sorry about that little incident, but don't give it another thought. We're better off this way. And it wouldn't be very nice for you to have your girlfriend see this –
   (*Pause.*)

SECOND CHAP: Miss Suzana isn't at home, then?
   (LEOPOLD *shrugs.*)

FIRST CHAP: We know she's at the cinema –
   (LEOPOLD *shrugs.*)

SECOND CHAP: Won't you talk to us?
   (LEOPOLD *shrugs.*)

FIRST CHAP: What are you writing at the moment, may one ask?

LEOPOLD: What does it matter –

FIRST CHAP: No harm in asking –
   (*Pause.*)

SECOND CHAP: When was the last time you went out?

LEOPOLD: I don't know –

FIRST CHAP: It was some time ago, wasn't it?

LEOPOLD: Hm –

(*Pause.* FIRST CHAP *looks through the medicines which are lying on the table.*)

FIRST CHAP: Vitamins?

LEOPOLD: Yes –

SECOND CHAP: Apart from vitamins are you on anything?

LEOPOLD: Not really – why?

FIRST CHAP: There's been some talk –

LEOPOLD: What sort of talk?

FIRST CHAP: Forget it –

(*Pause.*)

SECOND CHAP: How much do you drink?

LEOPOLD: The same as everyone else –

SECOND CHAP: Starting in the morning?

LEOPOLD: As the case may be –

(*Pause.*)

FIRST CHAP: Well look, Professor, we won't drag this out unnecessarily. We're here because we've been given the job of putting a proposition to you –

LEOPOLD: A proposition?

FIRST CHAP: Yes. As you know only too well, you're being threatened with something unpleasant which I personally wouldn't wish upon you and I don't suppose you are particularly looking forward to it yourself –

LEOPOLD: In a way it might be better than –

SECOND CHAP: Now, now, Professor, no blasphemy!

FIRST CHAP: As you've been told many times before, it's not our business to push these things to extremes – on the contrary we want to avoid confrontations, so that – if possible – things don't come to the worst –

SECOND CHAP: It's not in our interests –

FIRST CHAP: And in some cases, when there is no better alternative, we even look for ways to achieve our object without having to go down every twist and turn of the path –

SECOND CHAP: We always try to give people another chance –

FIRST CHAP: And that's why we're here. We've been given the job of notifying you that under certain conditions this whole matter could be dropped –

LEOPOLD: Dropped? How?

28

SECOND CHAP: The whole thing would be declared null and void.

LEOPOLD: Under what conditions?

FIRST CHAP: As you know, what's coming to you is coming to you because under the name of Professor Leopold Nettles you put together a certain paper –

SECOND CHAP: An essay, as you call it –

FIRST CHAP: You never denied it and in effect therefore, you brought the whole thing upon yourself – by this act of non-denial, you unmasked the perpetrator –
(*Brief pause.*)

SECOND CHAP: As a man of wide knowledge you must be aware that if the perpetrator isn't known one cannot proceed against him. This is known as the Principle of the Identity of the Perpetrator –

FIRST CHAP: In a word, if you would sign, here and now, a short statement saying that you are not Professor Leopold Nettles, author of the paper in question, then the whole thing will be considered null and void and all previous decisions rescinded –

LEOPOLD: If I understand you correctly you want me to declare that I am no longer me –

FIRST CHAP: That's a way of putting it which might do for a philosopher but of course from a legal point of view it doesn't make sense. Obviously it is not a matter of you declaring that you are no longer you, but only declaring that you are not the same person who is the author of that thing – essentially it's a formality –

SECOND CHAP: One name being like another name –

FIRST CHAP: Or do you think that Nettles is such a beautiful name that you couldn't bear to lose it? You only have to look in the phone book to see how many equally nice names there are –

SECOND CHAP:⎫
FIRST CHAP: ⎬ And most of them even nicer –

LEOPOLD: Do you mean that I have to change my name?

SECOND CHAP: Not at all! You can have whatever name you like, that's entirely up to you – nobody – at least in this instance – could care less. The only thing which is important here is whether you are or are not the Nettles who wrote that paper –

FIRST CHAP: If you insist on keeping your name for sentimental reasons then by all means keep it –

SECOND CHAP: Though there's no denying that it would be neater if you were to decide otherwise –

FIRST CHAP: It would be neater but it's not essential. After all there could be more than one Leopold Nettles –

SECOND CHAP: There are three just in the phone book –

FIRST CHAP: In other words, it is not so much a question of whether you are Nettles or Nichols but rather whether you are the Nettles who wrote the paper –

SECOND CHAP: You have to admit it's a good offer –

LEOPOLD: I don't understand what you'll achieve by it – or why, in that case, you're proposing it – as far as I know you never do anything without a reason –

FIRST CHAP: Our interest is to wipe this unpleasant business off the slate and give you one more chance –

LEOPOLD: What chance?

FIRST CHAP: To keep out of trouble until the next time –

LEOPOLD: I don't like it much –

FIRST CHAP: Now look, whether you like it or not is your own affair. Nobody is forcing you to do anything, and nobody can force you. But I'm telling you man to man that you'd be making a mistake if you didn't go along with it –

SECOND CHAP: It's a free gift!

FIRST CHAP: No one will know a thing so long as you don't go prattling on about it, and even if it gets around everyone will understand why you did it –

SECOND CHAP: They'd all do exactly the same –

FIRST CHAP: Many of them have already done it – and what harm has it done them? None –

SECOND CHAP: If you're hesitating then the only explanation I can think of is that you have no idea what's coming to you – (*Pause.*)

LEOPOLD: Would I have to do it right this minute?

FIRST CHAP: It would be best of course –

LEOPOLD: No, – this is definitely serious enough to require some reflection –

SECOND CHAP: If you want to take the risk –

LEOPOLD: What risk?

FIRST CHAP: Look, we've been given the job of notifying you of what we have notified you. We don't make the decisions –

SECOND CHAP: We're small fry –

FIRST CHAP: And we can't be expected to know, of course, what the relevant authorities will make of this whole business –

SECOND CHAP: All we can do is pass on your request for time to consider –

LEOPOLD: But surely it can't make much difference to them whether it's going to be today or the day after tomorrow!

FIRST CHAP: You must understand that their goodwill is not some kind of balloon which can be expanded indefinitely –

LEOPOLD: I do understand –

(*Longer pause.* LEOPOLD *has been rattled by all this and furthermore he's evidently becoming cold again in spite of the fact that he is wrapped up in the blanket. After a while the* SECOND CHAP *suddenly says in a loud voice.*)

SECOND CHAP: Don't be a fool, man! Here's a chance – with one stroke of the pen – to rid yourself of everything that's piled on your head, all the shit – a chance for a completely fresh start, it's once in a lifetime! What would I give for such a chance!

(*Short pause.* LEOPOLD *is openly trembling, either from nervousness or the cold.*)

LEOPOLD: (*Whispering*) Let's have a look –

(*The* SECOND CHAP *at once begins to go through all his pockets until finally in his back trouser pocket he finds a soiled piece of paper. He puts it on the table and straightens it out with the back of his hand. Then he gives it to* LEOPOLD *who holds it for a long time in his trembling hands and reads it carefully. After a while he slowly puts it back on the table and wraps himself up even more tightly in his blanket. Pause.*)

FIRST CHAP: Well, what's it to be?

(*The curtain falls, the music returns.*)

31

SCENE FIVE

The music fades as the curtain rises.

LEOPOLD is alone on stage. He paces the length of the room as a prisoner might pace his cell, back and forth between the front door and the bathroom door. When he reaches the front door for the third time he pauses and looks through the peep-hole. Then he puts his ear to the door and listens intently for a moment, and then continues walking. He paces back and forth twice more and then on reaching the door he pauses, reflects a moment, then goes to one of the bookcases and from behind some books he pulls out a wooden box. He takes it to the table, sits down on a chair and opens the box. It is full of various medicines. LEOPOLD starts going through them, then he considers a moment, hesitates, and prepares himself a dose from several of the medicines. He tosses the dose back into his mouth, takes a drink of rum and swallows the lot. He shuts the box, puts it back behind the books and continues to pace. When he comes to the bathroom door for the second time he pauses, considers a moment, and then goes into the bathroom leaving the door open. There is the sound of running water and LEOPOLD gasping. Evidently he is washing his face. After a while he re-enters, his face already dry, and closes the bathroom door and continues to pace. Reaching the front door for the third time he stops and looks through the peep-hole. He then puts his ear to the door, listening intently for a while, and then continues to pace. When he reaches the front door for the second time, he pauses, considers a moment, and then goes to the bookcase where his medicines are hidden and once more takes out his box. He takes it to the table, sits down on a chair and opens the box. He starts going through his medicines, considers a moment, hesitates, prepares himself another dose of various medicines, tosses the whole lot back into his mouth, takes a drink of rum and swallows the lot. He shuts the box, puts it back behind the books and continues to pace. When he reaches the bathroom door for the second time, he pauses, considers a moment and then goes into the bathroom leaving the door open. There is the sound of running water and LEOPOLD gasping. He is washing his face again. After a while he re-enters, his face already dry, closes the bathroom door and continues to pace. Reaching the front door for the third time he stops, considers a

*moment, looks through the peep-hole, steps quickly to the place where
his medicines are hidden, takes out his box, takes out one bottle of
medicine, empties it into his mouth and runs into the bathroom
leaving the door open. There is the sound of running water and*
LEOPOLD *gasping.* LEOPOLD *re-enters after a moment, closes the
bathroom door and goes quickly to the front door. He puts his ear to
the door, listens for a while and suddenly leaps back. At the same
moment a key rattles in the lock and through the front door comes*
SUZANA *carrying a full shopping bag.*

SUZANA: Hello –

LEOPOLD: Hello –

SUZANA: Isn't Edward here?

LEOPOLD: He hasn't come yet –

> (LEOPOLD *takes the shopping bag from* SUZANA, *carries it into
> the kitchen and immediately returns.*)

Did you get any vegetables?

SUZANA: A cauliflower –

LEOPOLD: You didn't!

> (SUZANA *goes up the little staircase to her room.* LEOPOLD
> *approaches the staircase, hesitating for a moment.*)

LEOPOLD: Suzana –

> (*She stops halfway up the staircase and turns towards him.*)

SUZANA: Yes?

LEOPOLD: They were here –

SUZANA: (*Surprised*) They were?

LEOPOLD: Yes –

SUZANA: When?

LEOPOLD: During the night –

SUZANA: And how come you're here?

LEOPOLD: I'll explain –

SUZANA: Did you promise them anything?

LEOPOLD: No –

SUZANA: You didn't get into trouble again in some way, did
you?

LEOPOLD: No –

SUZANA: What happened, then?

LEOPOLD: When you went out to the cinema with Edward,
Lucy and I cooked ourselves that liver –

SUZANA: Cooked it in what?

LEOPOLD: In a frying pan –

SUZANA: Which one?

LEOPOLD: The new one –

SUZANA: And you left it in a mess –

LEOPOLD: We scrubbed it –

SUZANA: With what?

LEOPOLD: With washing powder –

SUZANA: I might have known! You know very well you shouldn't use washing powder on it –

LEOPOLD: It's all right, you can have a look – then we talked for a while and then Bertram turned up, apparently on behalf of several friends – he said they were concerned about me – that I was in a bad way – that my home life was in a mess – that I was erratic – that I wasn't doing anything –

SUZANA: I've been telling you that for ages –

LEOPOLD: When Bertram left, Lucy and I had a bit of a row –

SUZANA: What about?

LEOPOLD: It's complicated – basically she complains that I don't love her enough – that I'm evasive – that I don't make it clear in company that we belong to each other, and so on – and when I honestly tried to explain things to her she said I was making excuses –

SUZANA: Well, does that surprise you?

LEOPOLD: I know what she means but what am I supposed to do?

SUZANA: Well, if you don't know –

LEOPOLD: Before she could leave they came and then because she insisted on staying they called some men in and they dragged her away –

SUZANA: Is she out yet?

LEOPOLD: I don't know – perhaps –

SUZANA: What do you mean, you don't know? Haven't you gone to see her?

LEOPOLD: I can't possibly leave here! Not now!

SUZANA: Of course. And what about them?

LEOPOLD: Apparently I won't have to go there if I make a statement that I am not the author of that – if I say simply

34

that I am somebody else –

SUZANA: Somebody else! That would just suit them! Denounce
yourself and spit on your own work!

LEOPOLD: They are not asking me to make a value judgement,
they only want a formal excuse to drop the whole thing –

SUZANA: Tsss!

LEOPOLD: They're obviously worried that once I get there it
would only increase the respect in which I'm held –

SUZANA: Whereas if you were to recant you'd lose it all!
Obviously that would be much more to their liking! I hope
you threw them out –

LEOPOLD: I've asked for time to consider –

SUZANA: What?

LEOPOLD: There's nothing to it, surely –

SUZANA: Have you gone mad? What is there to consider? That's
just showing them that they're half way to breaking you –
and now they'll increase the pressure! I knew as soon as I
saw you that you'd got yourself into trouble! You wet!

LEOPOLD: It's all very well for you to talk –

SUZANA: If you can't take it you should never have got into it.

(SUZANA *turns abruptly and goes towards her room.*)

LEOPOLD: Suzana –

SUZANA: (*Without looking at him*) Leave me alone –

(SUZANA *goes into her room.* LEOPOLD *nervously begins to
pace his usual path. When he reaches the front door for the third
time, he stops, goes to the spot where his medicines are hidden,
quickly extracts his box, takes a pill out of a bottle, throws it
into his mouth and swallows it. He puts the box back, then
continues pacing and when he gets to the bathroom door he
pauses, goes quickly to the front door, looks through the peep-
hole and then runs into the bathroom leaving the door open.
There is the sound of running water and* LEOPOLD's *gasping.
Suddenly the doorbell rings. Water is still running,* LEOPOLD *is
gasping and obviously does not hear the bell. After a while the
bell rings again. The sound of running water stops, and after a
moment* LEOPOLD *comes out of the bathroom, drying his wet
hair with a towel. Drying his hair he continues to pace. When
he reaches the front door for the third time he looks through the*

peep-hole. At that moment the bell rings again. LEOPOLD *jumps, then he returns to the door and looks through the peep-hole. He calms down and looks through the door.* EDWARD *enters wearing a dinner jacket.*)

EDWARD: At last!

LEOPOLD: Has something happened?

EDWARD: I rang three times –

LEOPOLD: I was getting myself together –

EDWARD: (*Going to the balcony door*) Can I open it a bit?

LEOPOLD: Go ahead.

(EDWARD *opens the balcony door wide.* LEOPOLD, *the towel round his neck, walks slowly round the room.* EDWARD *sits down on a chair.*)

EDWARD: I'm relieved to find you here –

LEOPOLD: You know, then?

EDWARD: Lucy came to see me –

LEOPOLD: So she's out –

EDWARD: What did they want?

LEOPOLD: To negotiate –

EDWARD: Did you sign anything?

LEOPOLD: I've asked for time to consider –

EDWARD: When will they be back?

LEOPOLD: They never say –

EDWARD: You ought to go and see Lucy, she's having a bad time one way and another –

LEOPOLD: I can't possibly leave here! Not now!

EDWARD: Is Suzana at home?

LEOPOLD: Yes – she was just asking for you –

(LEOPOLD *goes into the bathroom and after a while returns without the towel and with his hair combed.*)

Do you mind if I close it now?

EDWARD: Leave it a while –

(LEOPOLD *returns to his place and sits down. Pause.*)

LEOPOLD: That's a nice outfit you've got on –

EDWARD: It's a dinner jacket – my uncle lent it to me –

LEOPOLD: I know it's a dinner jacket – it's nice –

EDWARD: You know my uncle – (*Pause.*) How did you sleep?

LEOPOLD: Hardly at all –

36

EDWARD: You couldn't get them out of your mind, could you?

LEOPOLD: Well –

(*Pause.*)

EDWARD: Did you go this morning?

LEOPOLD: Yes –

EDWARD: Well, that's something anyway –

LEOPOLD: Not much of a thing, as it happens –

(*Pause.*)

EDWARD: What did you eat?

LEOPOLD: I wasn't hungry, I just ate a couple of onions and five almonds to calm myself down –

EDWARD: And did it?

LEOPOLD: Not really –

(*Pause.*)

EDWARD: The main thing is that you're here –

LEOPOLD: I'd rather be there than here like this! Why can't I get my life clear! It was wonderful when nobody was interested in me – when nobody expected anything from me, nobody urging me to do anything – I just browsed around the second-hand bookshops – studying the modern philosophers at my leisure – spending the nights making notes from their works – taking walks in the parks and meditating – why can't I change my name to Nichols, say, and forget everything and start a completely new life?

EDWARD: Perhaps you need some of your pills –

LEOPOLD: I splash water on my face – I don't want pills – I don't want to get dependent on them –

(*Pause.* LEOPOLD *becomes alert, and listening.*)

EDWARD: Nothing –

(*At that moment the doorbell rings.* LEOPOLD *jumps up in confusion.* EDWARD *also gets up.* LEOPOLD *goes to the peep-hole and looks through it and leaps back from the door and runs across the room into the bathroom leaving the door open. Immediately there is the sound of running water.* EDWARD *is puzzled. He steps to the bathroom door. Short pause.*)

(*Whispering towards the bathroom*) Leopold, come on –

(*Short pause and the sound of water.*)

(*Whispering towards the bathroom*) Don't be silly, Leopold, face up to it!

(*Short pause and the sound of water.*)

(*Whispering towards the bathroom*) I'll tell them you're not at home if you like but it would be better to get it over with –

(*Short pause and the sound of water. The bell rings again.* EDWARD *doesn't know what to do. Then he makes up his mind abruptly and goes decisively to the main door, to the front door, opens it wide and gazes with surprise.* FIRST SIDNEY *and* SECOND SIDNEY *enter each carrying a large suitcase. They put their suitcases down.*)

FIRST SIDNEY: Good afternoon –

EDWARD: Good afternoon –

FIRST SIDNEY: Isn't the professor in?

(EDWARD *is puzzled. Finally he nods, slowly closes the door and goes into the bathroom leaving the door half open. There is a short pause. The sound of water stops suddenly and there is some incomprehensible whispering for quite a long time off stage.* FIRST SIDNEY *and* SECOND SIDNEY *stand motionless next to their suitcases. Finally* LEOPOLD *comes out of the bathroom with his hair wet but sleekly combed.* EDWARD *follows him, closing the bathroom door.*)

LEOPOLD: Good afternoon –

SECOND SIDNEY: Here we are, professor –

LEOPOLD: Excellent –

FIRST SIDNEY: We've got it –

LEOPOLD: What?

(FIRST SIDNEY *and* SECOND SIDNEY *put their suitcases on the table and open them. Both suitcases are full of various documents.*)

FIRST SIDNEY: (*Pointing to his suitcase*) These are blank papers – these are normal office issue – these are for carbon copies – these are carbon papers – and here we have various envelopes and files and so on –

LEOPOLD: Is that all for me?

FIRST SIDNEY: Of course –

LEOPOLD: How much do I owe you?

FIRST SIDNEY: Do me a favour, professor, what do you take us for!

LEOPOLD: Well, thank you very much – I think that should last me –

SECOND SIDNEY: We're looking forward to what you'll be writing on these bits of paper –

FIRST SIDNEY: (*Pointing to the other suitcase*) Well, and this is the stuff from our plant – these are minutes of the board of management – these are minutes of meetings of all the paper-mill employees – these are specimens of factory correspondence – here we have various memos, internal regulations, information for the work-force, overtime summaries – and this is specially interesting, that's from the personnel department – personal records of employees – various complaints – returns – denunciations –

SECOND SIDNEY: I think it'll make very nice reading for you –

FIRST SIDNEY: Use it as you see fit –

SECOND SIDNEY: If you can do anything with it, it will certainly be a bombshell –

FIRST SIDNEY: Absolutely –

LEOPOLD: Thank you so –

(FIRST SIDNEY *takes a sheaf of papers out of one of the suitcases and looks around.*)

FIRST SIDNEY: Where do you want it?

LEOPOLD: (*Looking around*) Where? Well, in this corner, here –

(LEOPOLD *points to the left-hand corner of the room, downstage.* FIRST SIDNEY *and* SECOND SIDNEY *start taking papers from the two suitcases and carrying them to the corner where they place them on the floor. After a while they are joined first by* LEOPOLD *and then by* EDWARD. *When the contents of both suitcases are in the corner,* SECOND SIDNEY *closes both of the now empty cases and carries them to the front door. Then* FIRST *and* SECOND SIDNEY *sit down at the table.* LEOPOLD *sits down on the sofa.* EDWARD *remains standing in the background. There is a long awkward pause.*)

LEOPOLD: There's a lot of it –

SECOND SIDNEY: For you we'd steal the whole paper mill if we had to –

LEOPOLD: Thank you –

(*Awkward pause.*)

39

I wasn't expecting you so soon –

FIRST SIDNEY: One must strike while the iron is hot, that's what me and Sidney always say –

LEOPOLD: Very well put –

(*Awkward pause.*)

I don't know how I'm ever going to repay you –

SECOND SIDNEY: What is there to repay? We've already told you that we're your fans – and not just us –

FIRST SIDNEY: There's lots of people looking to you –

LEOPOLD: Thank you –

(*Awkward pause.*)

I wasn't expecting you so soon –

SECOND SIDNEY: One must strike while the iron is hot, that's what me and Sidney always say –

LEOPOLD: Very well put –

(*Awkward pause.*)

I don't know how I'm ever going to repay you –

FIRST SIDNEY: What is there to repay? We've already told you that we're your fans – and not just us –

SECOND SIDNEY: There's lots of people looking to you –

(*Awkward pause.*)

LEOPOLD: I don't know how I'll ever repay you –

SECOND SIDNEY: What is there to repay? We've already told you that we're your fans – and not just us –

LEOPOLD: Excuse me –

(LEOPOLD *gets up and goes to the balcony door and closes it and then returns to his seat.* SECOND SIDNEY *is feeling his pockets.* LEOPOLD *offers him a cigarette.*)

SECOND SIDNEY: I've got some today –

(SECOND SIDNEY *finds his cigarettes at last and he lights one.*)

But could I ask you for something else –

LEOPOLD: I'm at your disposal –

SECOND SIDNEY: Would there be any chance of a glass of rum?

LEOPOLD: Yes – of course –

SECOND SIDNEY: Just to clarify – I'm a teetotaller – but I was asking for Sidney here – he drinks like a fish –

(LEOPOLD *gets up and goes to the kitchen and comes back at once with a glass. He pours rum from his bottle into the glass and hands it to* FIRST SIDNEY.)

FIRST SIDNEY: Thanks! Cheers!

(FIRST SIDNEY *drinks the whole glass in one go and then burps, satisfied.* LEOPOLD *refills his glass.*)

FIRST SIDNEY: Thanks! Cheers!

(FIRST SIDNEY *drinks the whole glass in one go and then burps, satisfied.* LEOPOLD *fills his glass again.*)

Thanks! Cheers!

(FIRST SIDNEY *drinks the whole glass in one go and then burps, satisfied.* SUZANA *comes out of her room in a long evening dress and walks down the little staircase.*)

LEOPOLD: Look, Suzana, these gentlemen have brought me all this paper and all sorts of interesting stuff –

SUZANA: Where's it going to go?

LEOPOLD: I'll find somewhere – that's a nice dress.

(SUZANA *makes a sign to* EDWARD *who accompanies her to the kitchen. During the rest of the scene both of them can be seen through the glass-panelled kitchen door taking out various foodstuffs from the shopping bag, putting them where they belong, and, during all this time either discussing something in a lively way or perhaps quarrelling.* LEOPOLD *notices that* FIRST SIDNEY*'s glass is empty and fills it up again for him.*)

FIRST SIDNEY: Thanks! Cheers!

(FIRST SIDNEY *drinks the whole glass in one go and then burps, satisfied.* LEOPOLD *refills the glass.*)

Thanks! Cheers!

(FIRST SIDNEY *drinks the whole glass in one go and then burps, satisfied.* LEOPOLD *refills the glass.*)

Thanks! Cheers!

(FIRST SIDNEY *drinks the whole glass in one go and then burps, satisfied.* LEOPOLD *refills the glass.*)

Thanks! Cheers!

(FIRST SIDNEY *drinks the whole glass in one go and then burps, satisfied.* LEOPOLD *refills the glass.* FIRST SIDNEY *takes the glass but when he is on the point of drinking it he puts it back on the table.*)

FIRST SIDNEY: Someone has to be sensible –

(*Short pause.*)

SECOND SIDNEY: We're not holding you up are we?

LEOPOLD: No –

FIRST SIDNEY: Are you sure? Because if we are you only have to say so and we'll push off –

LEOPOLD: You're not holding me up – excuse me –

(LEOPOLD *gets up, goes to the place where his medicines are hidden, turns his back to the room so as not to be seen, pulls out his box, quickly takes out a pill, throws it into his mouth and swallows it and puts his box back and returns to his seat. Pause.*)

SECOND SIDNEY: Have you thought about it yet?

LEOPOLD: About what?

FIRST SIDNEY: What we were talking about yesterday – that it's time for an initiative –

LEOPOLD: Oh yes – I haven't got round to it yet –

SECOND SIDNEY: Pity. You know, I'm an ordinary bloke, a nobody, but I can spot a few things and I've got my own opinion and nobody can deny me that. And what I think is, there's a lot that could be done – certainly more than is being done at the moment –

FIRST SIDNEY: One just has to get hold of the situation by the –

SECOND SIDNEY: Who else but you is there to get things going again?

(LEOPOLD *is starting to get nervous. He looks discreetly at his watch.*)

FIRST SIDNEY: We're not holding you up are we?

LEOPOLD: No –

SECOND SIDNEY: Are you sure? Because if we are you only have to say so and we'll push off –

LEOPOLD: You're not holding me up. Excuse me –

(LEOPOLD *gets up and goes into the bathroom, leaving the door open. There is the sound of running water and* LEOPOLD *gasping. The sound of water stops and shortly afterwards* LEOPOLD *returns to his seat.*)

FIRST SIDNEY: That thing you wrote – even if we don't fully understand it –

SECOND SIDNEY: We're ordinary people –

FIRST SIDNEY: – and the fact that you're right behind it –

SECOND SIDNEY: – regardless of the consequences –

FIRST SIDNEY: – straight away leads one to hope that you will take the final step –

LEOPOLD: What final step?

SECOND SIDNEY: I'm not really good at explaining myself but let me put it like this – that whatever you're writing, you'll turn it into something that will have a practical effect –

FIRST SIDNEY: To put it simply, that you'll come up with the pay-off to all your philosophizing –

LEOPOLD: The trouble is that opinions differ about quite what the pay-off is –

SECOND SIDNEY: You'll find it –

FIRST SIDNEY: Who else but you is there to get things going again –

SECOND SIDNEY: I'd say that's just what people are waiting for –

LEOPOLD: What people?

FIRST SIDNEY: Everybody –

LEOPOLD: Isn't that a bit of an exaggeration?

SECOND SIDNEY: Forgive me but you probably don't realize –

LEOPOLD: What?

FIRST SIDNEY: Your responsibility –

LEOPOLD: For what?

SECOND SIDNEY: For everything –

(LEOPOLD *is evidently nervous. He looks at his watch.*)

FIRST SIDNEY: We're not holding you up?

LEOPOLD: No –

FIRST SIDNEY:⎫ Are you sure? Because if we are you only
SECOND SIDNEY:⎭ have to say so and we'll push off –

LEOPOLD: You're not holding me up. Excuse me –

(LEOPOLD *gets up and goes to the kitchen and returns shortly with a small plate on which there are two onions and five almonds. He eats the lot during the following dialogue.*)

SECOND SIDNEY: Sidney and I were giving it a bit of thought the other day –

FIRST SIDNEY: And we got the following idea –

LEOPOLD: What idea?

SECOND SIDNEY: We think it's quite good –

LEOPOLD: What idea?

FIRST SIDNEY: This could be exactly the step that everyone is waiting for you to take –

LEOPOLD: What?

SECOND SIDNEY: That you should write a kind of declaration –

LEOPOLD: What kind of declaration?

FIRST SIDNEY: Quite simply a kind of general declaration covering all the basics –

SECOND SIDNEY: It would have to be brief and easy to understand of course –

FIRST SIDNEY: In other words you'd have to spend some time on it –

SECOND SIDNEY: You've got plenty of paper now –
    (LEOPOLD, *irritated, gets up, ambles round the room and then turns to the* TWO SIDNEYS.)

LEOPOLD: Forgive me, gentlemen, but I'm not clear about –
    (SUZANA, *followed by* EDWARD, *comes out of the kitchen.*
    LEOPOLD *looks at them in surprise.*)
    (*To* SUZANA) Are you leaving?

SUZANA: Why?

LEOPOLD: I thought that we might – since you got that cauliflower – since I need to calm down a bit – to examine everything calmly – to discuss –

SUZANA: Forgive me, Leopold, but I've got tickets for a dance – I bought them ages ago –

LEOPOLD: I see – I see –

SUZANA: It's my first dance this year –

LEOPOLD: I understand – I understand –

SUZANA: Not that I know what there is to discuss – I've already given you my opinion –

LEOPOLD: I know – I only thought – but it doesn't really matter –

SUZANA: Well, so long –

EDWARD: So long, Leopold – and get to bed soon – get some sleep –
    (SUZANA *and* EDWARD *leave through the front door.*
    LEOPOLD *looks at them awkwardly as they leave. Pause.*)

FIRST SIDNEY: What aren't you clear about?

LEOPOLD: (*Turning round*) I beg your pardon?

SECOND SIDNEY: You were saying that you weren't clear about something –

44

LEOPOLD: Was I? Ah – yes – don't be angry, gentlemen, but I'm not really quite clear about –

FIRST SIDNEY: About what?

LEOPOLD: About what exactly you want from me –

(FIRST SIDNEY *drinks the glass of rum in one go and then gets up.* SECOND SIDNEY *gets up also. They both step nearer to* LEOPOLD.)

FIRST SIDNEY: Professor, you've obviously got us wrong – we don't want anything from you –

SECOND SIDNEY: We've only taken the liberty of giving you our opinion –

FIRST SIDNEY: It's the opinion of ordinary people –

SECOND SIDNEY: Of lots of ordinary people –

FIRST SIDNEY: We only wanted to offer a suggestion –

SECOND SIDNEY: We meant well –

FIRST SIDNEY: We can't help not being able to express ourselves exactly –

SECOND SIDNEY: We're not philosophers –

FIRST SIDNEY: We just thought you might be interested in our opinion –

SECOND SIDNEY: As representing the opinion of ordinary –

LEOPOLD: I'm not saying that I'm not interested in your opinion –

FIRST SIDNEY: Well, you seem to be implying that we're confusing you –

LEOPOLD: Really I'm not suggesting anything of the sort –

SECOND SIDNEY: You were saying that you weren't clear about what we want from you –

LEOPOLD: I don't exactly know what I was saying –

FIRST SIDNEY: But we know –

(*At that moment the bathroom door opens.* BERTRAM *is standing in the doorway talking to* LEOPOLD.)

BERTRAM: I don't want to be hard on you or hurt you in any way.

(*At that moment the kitchen door opens.* EDWARD *is standing there speaking to* LEOPOLD.)

EDWARD: Were you worried?

(*At that moment the door of Suzana's room opens.* SUZANA *is standing there speaking to* LEOPOLD.)

SUZANA: Are you sure you didn't get yourself into trouble again somehow?

BERTRAM: I'm not just speaking for myself.

EDWARD: Perhaps you should take some pills –

(*At that moment the balcony door opens.* LUCY *is standing there in her bedspread and speaking to* LEOPOLD.)

LUCY: You sang a different tune the first time you got me to stay here with you.

EDWARD: You ought to go and see Lucy.

FIRST SIDNEY: This could be what people are waiting for –

SECOND SIDNEY: You'll find a way –

SUZANA: What is there to consider, for goodness sake.

BERTRAM: And how are things between you and Suzana?

LUCY: You've had enough of me and now you want to get shot of me –

EDWARD: Did you sign anything?

FIRST SIDNEY: We've only taken the liberty of giving you our opinion –

SECOND SIDNEY: The opinion of ordinary people –

FIRST SIDNEY: Lots of ordinary people –

EDWARD: Some hero.

SUZANA: Some hero.

BERTRAM: Some hero.

LUCY: Some hero.

FIRST SIDNEY: You've had enough of me and now you want to get shot of me.

SECOND SIDNEY: Some hero.

FIRST SIDNEY: Did you sign anything?

LEOPOLD: (*Shouting*) GET OUT!

(*For a moment there is complete silence and then the doorbell rings.* LEOPOLD *runs into the bathroom.* BERTRAM *makes way for him and* LEOPOLD *disappears into the bathroom and immediately there is the sound of running water. All the people on stage disappear behind the doors through which they came.* FIRST *and* SECOND SIDNEY *disappear with their suitcases through the front door. They all go and all the doors except the bathroom door are closed. The only sound is running water and*

46

LEOPOLD *gasping. The doorbell rings again.*
The curtain falls as the music begins to be heard.)

SCENE SIX

The music fades as the curtain rises.
   *There is no one on the stage. The bathroom door is open. There is
the sound of running water and of* LEOPOLD *gasping. There is a
short pause. Then the bell rings. The sound of water stops and*
LEOPOLD *runs out of the bathroom. He was obviously having a
shower. He is wet and is covered only by a towel wrapped round his
waist. He runs to the main door, looks through the peep-hole, is
taken aback, hesitates a moment and then opens the door.*
MARGUERITE *enters.*
MARGUERITE: Good evening –
LEOPOLD: (*A bit nonplussed*) Good evening –
   (*Short pause.*)
MARGUERITE: Professor Nettles?
LEOPOLD: Yes –
   (*Short pause.*)
MARGUERITE: Sorry to disturb you –
LEOPOLD: You're not disturbing me –
MARGUERITE: I won't hold you up for long –
LEOPOLD: I've got time –
   (*Short pause.*)
MARGUERITE: My name's Marguerite. I'm a student of
   philosophy –
LEOPOLD: At the university or a private student?
MARGUERITE: Both –
   (MARGUERITE *walks to the middle of the room and looks
   round uncertainly.* LEOPOLD *closes the door. A short pause.*)
   Sit down –
MARGUERITE: Thank you –
   (MARGUERITE *sits down shyly on the edge of the sofa.*)
LEOPOLD: Would you like some rum?
MARGUERITE: No – thank you – I'm not used to rum –
LEOPOLD: One glass won't do you any harm –

47

(LEOPOLD *pours some rum into the glass which has remained on the table.*)

MARGUERITE: Well, thank you –

(MARGUERITE *takes a very small sip and winces.*)

LEOPOLD: Not bad is it?

MARGUERITE: No –

(*Awkward pause.*)

You'll catch cold.

LEOPOLD: Ah yes, of course –

(LEOPOLD *goes quickly into the bathroom and comes back in a moment wearing a dressing gown under which he is naked. He sits down on the sofa next to* MARGUERITE *and smiles at her.* MARGUERITE *smiles back. There is a longer awkward pause.*)

MARGUERITE: I know your work –

LEOPOLD: Really? Which?

MARGUERITE: *Phenomenology of Responsibility, Love and Nothingness, Ontology of the Human Self* –

LEOPOLD: You've read all those?

MARGUERITE: Several times –

LEOPOLD: Well, I am impressed –

(*Pause.*)

MARGUERITE: I hear *Ontology of the Human Self* got you into trouble –

LEOPOLD: It's because of that I'm supposed to go there –

MARGUERITE: What – straight there? How come?

LEOPOLD: Paragraph 511 – intellectual hooliganism –

MARGUERITE: That's awful!

LEOPOLD: That's the sort of world we're living in –

MARGUERITE: For such beautiful thoughts!

LEOPOLD: Apparently someone didn't think they were so beautiful –

MARGUERITE: And is it definite?

LEOPOLD: I could get out of it by denying that I wrote it –

MARGUERITE: Is that what they're offering you?

LEOPOLD: Yes –

MARGUERITE: They're disgusting!

(*Pause.* MARGUERITE *takes a sip and winces.* LEOPOLD *promptly fills up her glass.*)

Your essays have given me a great deal of –

LEOPOLD: Yes? I'm so glad –

MARGUERITE: It's because of them that I became interested in philosophy –

LEOPOLD: Really?

MARGUERITE: Somehow they opened my eyes –

LEOPOLD: You're exaggerating –

MARGUERITE: Really –

LEOPOLD: Have another drink –

(MARGUERITE *has a drink and winces.* LEOPOLD *promptly refills her glass. Awkward pause.*)

MARGUERITE: Are you writing anything?

LEOPOLD: I'm trying to –

MARGUERITE: Could you tell me – excuse my curiosity – could you tell me what you're writing?

LEOPOLD: I'm trying to think about love as a dimension of being –

MARGUERITE: You touched on that a little in the second chapter of *Love and Nothingness* –

LEOPOLD: That's right –
    (*Awkward pause.*)

MARGUERITE: Professor –

LEOPOLD: Yes, Marguerite?

MARGUERITE: I wouldn't dare to trouble you –

LEOPOLD: You're not troubling me at all! On the contrary – I'm very pleased to have met you –

MARGUERITE: If it wasn't for the fact that I'm sure you're the only one who can help me –

LEOPOLD: What's the matter?

MARGUERITE: It's going to sound silly –

LEOPOLD: You can tell me!

MARGUERITE: I'm suddenly embarrassed –

LEOPOLD: But why, there's no need –
    (MARGUERITE *has a drink and winces.* LEOPOLD *promptly refills her glass. Short pause.*)

MARGUERITE: Where should I begin? I just don't know what to do –

LEOPOLD: In your studies?

49

MARGUERITE: In my life –

LEOPOLD: In your life?

MARGUERITE: I find everything so stifling – all those hopeless faces in the bus queues – the endless hue and cry in the streets – people twisted out of shape in their offices and everywhere else – the general misery of life – forgive me, I know it's silly, you don't even know me – but I didn't know anyone else I could turn to –

LEOPOLD: I'm delighted that you should confide in me –

MARGUERITE: I don't get on with my parents – they're middle class types who are always watching TV – I've no boyfriend – the other students seem terribly superficial –

LEOPOLD: I know what you mean –

MARGUERITE: You're not angry?

LEOPOLD: Why do you make excuses for yourself all the time? What greater satisfaction could there be for a philosopher than to receive a visit from a reader in mid-crisis about the meaning of life?

MARGUERITE: I know that you can't solve my problem for me –

LEOPOLD: You're right in the sense that the meaning of life is not something which one can summarize or verbalize one way or the other and then hand over like a piece of information – it's not an object, it's more like an elusive spiritual state – and the more one needs it the more elusive it becomes –

MARGUERITE: Yes, yes, that's exactly –

LEOPOLD: On the other hand there is the fact – as I've already tried to show in *Ontology of the Human Self* – that there's a certain non-verbal, existential space in which – and only in which – one can get hold of something through experiencing the presence of another person –

MARGUERITE: Forgive me, it's exactly that part – it's from chapter four – which made me decide to come and see you –

LEOPOLD: There you are! But I wouldn't like to raise your hopes unduly, because the fact that I'm meditating on this subject doesn't automatically mean that I am myself capable of creating such a space –

MARGUERITE: But you've been creating it for ages – by talking

50

to me at all – by understanding me – forgive me, I'm
probably already a bit tipsy –

LEOPOLD: Not at all! Drink up –

(MARGUERITE *takes a drink and winces.* LEOPOLD *promptly
fills up her glass.*)

LEOPOLD: I'll tell you something, Marguerite – honesty deserves
honesty: if I am able to understand you then it is mainly
because I'm in a similar or perhaps even worse situation than
you –

MARGUERITE: You? I can't believe it! You know so much –
you've achieved so much – you're so wise –

LEOPOLD: That guarantees nothing –

MARGUERITE: I'm only a silly girl, but you –

LEOPOLD: You're not silly –

MARGUERITE: I am, I know it –

LEOPOLD: You're clever, Marguerite – and not only that, you're
beautiful –

MARGUERITE: Me? Well, whatever next –

LEOPOLD: I'll be quite frank with you, Marguerite: I'm in a very
bad way –

MARGUERITE: I know life has been hard on you but you seem so
strong –

LEOPOLD: Alas, that's only appearance. In reality I've had the
feeling for some time now that something is collapsing inside
me – as if an axis holding me together has started to break –
the ground crumbling under my feet – I lack a fixed point
from which everything inside me could grow and develop – I
get the feeling sometimes that I'm not really doing anything
except listening helplessly to the time going by. Gone is the
perspective I once had – my humour – my industry and
persistence – the pointedness of my observations –

MARGUERITE: How beautifully you put it –

LEOPOLD: You should have known me before! It's all gone, my
irony, my self-irony, my capacity for enthusiasm, for
emotional involvement, for commitment, even for sacrifice!
This might disappoint you, Marguerite, but for a long time I
haven't been the person that you obviously take me for!
Basically I'm a tired, dried out, broken man –

MARGUERITE: You mustn't speak like that, Professor! You're too hard on yourself! But even if it were all true the very fact that you are reflecting upon your situation shows that all is not lost –

LEOPOLD: You're good to me, Marguerite! And please don't call me professor, it sounds so formal! Why aren't you drinking?

(MARGUERITE *has a drink and winces.* LEOPOLD *promptly fills up her glass. Short pause.*)

MARGUERITE: So many people think so highly of you! Doesn't that alone give you strength?

LEOPOLD: On the contrary! I often say to myself how wonderful it was when nobody was interested in me – when nobody expected anything from me and nobody was urging me to do things – I used to browse around the second-hand bookshops – studying modern philosophers at my leisure – spending the nights making notes from their works – taking walks in the parks and meditating –

MARGUERITE: But it's thanks to all that that you are what you are today –

LEOPOLD: That's true, but it's also true that I've taken upon myself a heavier burden than I'm able to bear –

MARGUERITE: Leopold, I believe that you will win through!

LEOPOLD: I have a feeling that my only way out is to accept a term there – somewhere far away from my nearest and dearest – and put my humble trust in a higher will, to give me the chance to atone for my guilt – to lose my apathy and regain my pride – and as a nameless cog in a giant machine to purify myself – thus and only thus – If I manage to drain the bitter cup with dignity – I can get back – perhaps – something of my lost human integrity – renew the hope inside me – reconstitute myself emotionally – open the door to a new life –

MARGUERITE: (*Shouts*) But Leopold!

LEOPOLD: Yes?

MARGUERITE: (*Excitedly*) Don't you see that the punishment is deeply unjust and if you try – however honourably – to turn it into a purifying experience you'd just be agreeing with it and so prostrating yourself before it. And what's more, by giving it this so-called meaning you're hiding from yourself the fact that you're clinging to it as a kind of escape from your life, a way out of your problems. But however far they send you, punishment won't solve what you can't solve yourself! Don't you understand that you've done nothing and so there is nothing to atone! You're innocent!

LEOPOLD: Oh, Marguerite – why didn't I meet you before it was too late?

(LEOPOLD *takes hold of her hands and kisses them.*
MARGUERITE *is embarrassed.* LEOPOLD *holds her hands. She drops her eyes. Long pause*)

MARGUERITE: (*Whispering*) Leopold –

LEOPOLD: Yes –

MARGUERITE: Do you love anybody?

LEOPOLD: Ah, my dear girl, I really don't know if I'm capable of love –

MARGUERITE: Don't tell me that you've never felt anything towards a woman –

LEOPOLD: Nervousness – more with some, less with others –

MARGUERITE: You need love! Mad passionate true love! Didn't you yourself write in *Phenomenology of Responsibility* that a person who doesn't love doesn't exist? Only love will give you the strength to stand up to them!

LEOPOLD: That's easy for you to say, Marguerite, but where would one find it?

(MARGUERITE *takes a quick drink, winces and quietly blurts out.*)

MARGUERITE: With me!

LEOPOLD: What? You?

MARGUERITE: (*Excited*) Yes! You have given me back the meaning to my life, which is to give you the meaning back to yours! I'll save you!

(LEOPOLD *strokes her hair.*)

LEOPOLD: You're wonderful, Marguerite! But I can't allow you to throw your life away on someone as worthless as myself –

MARGUERITE: On the contrary I would be fulfilling my life!

LEOPOLD: Apart from the fact that I'm an old man –

53

MARGUERITE: That's nonsense! I've made up my mind –

LEOPOLD: If I'd known it would come to this I'd never have told you my problems –

MARGUERITE: Thank goodness you did! I'll give you back strength – courage – self-confidence – joy – appetite for life! I'll bring your failing heart back to life! I know you're capable of love! How else could you have written those things! I'll bring you back to life and at the same time back to philosophy!

(LEOPOLD *takes hold of* MARGUERITE'*s arms and for a moment looks deeply into her eyes and then begins to kiss her rapidly over her face and neck.*)

MARGUERITE: Ah – Leopold – ah – I love you – I love your thoughts and your words – you awoke my love a long time ago without knowing it – without my knowing it – and now I'll awaken love in you!

(*At that moment the doorbell rings.* LEOPOLD *jumps up at once.*)

LEOPOLD: (*Whispering*) Quick – go out on the balcony!

MARGUERITE: (*Whispering*) Why?

LEOPOLD: (*Whispering*) They'll drag you off!

(LEOPOLD *takes her by the hand and hurries her to the balcony door. He opens the door and pushes her on to the balcony and closes the door. He runs into the bedroom leaving the door open. Pause. The doorbell rings again. Pause. Then* LEOPOLD, *grey-faced, emerges from the bedroom wearing a suit and an overcoat and carrying a small military valise. He goes to the front door. Opens it bravely.* FIRST CHAP *and* SECOND CHAP *enter.* LEOPOLD *closes the door behind them.*)

FIRST CHAP: On your own today?

LEOPOLD: (*Bravely*) Gentlemen! Do your duty! I'll get ready!

SECOND CHAP: What's the hurry? It may not come to the worst –

(*The* FIRST CHAP *goes to the balcony door, opens it and says:*)

FIRST CHAP: Come in, my little one –

(MARGUERITE *slowly enters the room.*)

LEOPOLD: Don't you dare touch her! If you drag her off, then –

SECOND CHAP: Then what?

LEOPOLD: Then – then –

FIRST CHAP: Don't you worry, there's no need for her to go anywhere. Today there'd be no point –

LEOPOLD: You're right. As you're obviously aware, I'm not going to sign that statement. I'd rather die than give up my own human identity – it's the only thing I've got!

SECOND CHAP: But Professor, why are you carrying on like this? You're not going anywhere –

LEOPOLD: Why not? I've told you quite clearly that I'm not going to sign anything! I'm not guilty!

FIRST CHAP: You don't have to sign anything! Your case has been adjourned indefinitely –

SECOND CHAP: Indefinitely for the time being.

FIRST CHAP: For the time being.

SECOND CHAP: Without signature!

LEOPOLD: What? Adjourned?

FIRST CHAP: That's right. Adjourned!

LEOPOLD: You mean no signature and no *there* either?

SECOND CHAP: For the time being, mind, for the time being –

LEOPOLD: I don't understand what it means – why don't you want my signature any more?

FIRST CHAP: It would be just a formality. Who needs it? It's become pretty clear by now that in your case it would be superfluous –

LEOPOLD: Are you trying to say that I am no longer me?

SECOND CHAP: You said it, not me.

(*Short pause.* LEOPOLD *gazes at the* FIRST *and* SECOND CHAP *and then shouts.*)

LEOPOLD: I don't want an adjournment! I want to go there!
(LEOPOLD *suddenly falls to his knees in front of the* CHAPS *and starts to sob.*)
I'm begging you – I beseech you – I can't go on living like this –

FIRST CHAP: It seems you'll have to –

MARGUERITE: (*Calling to him*) Leopold get up! You're not going to beg them, are you!

LEOPOLD: (*Shouting at* MARGUERITE) Leave me alone! All of you leave me alone!

55

(LEOPOLD *collapses on the floor, banging his fists on it. The curtain falls and the music returns.*)

SCENE SEVEN

The music is fading and the curtain begins to rise slowly. LEOPOLD *is alone on the stage. He is sitting on the sofa staring at the front door. After a longer pause he gets up and goes to the door and looks through the peep-hole. Then he puts his ear to the door and listens intently. The lights start to come up in the auditorium and the music begins to be heard.* LEOPOLD *straightens up slowly, goes to the footlights and bows. At the same time all the other characters enter from the various doors and gather round* LEOPOLD *bowing.*

    The curtain falls.

END